Paul, a servant of Christ Jesus
and an apostle chosen and called
by God to preach his Good News.
From the Letter to the Romans

# THE LIFE AND LETTERS OF PAUL

Compiled by Pat Alexander
Photographs by Sonia Halliday and Laura Lushington

SANDY LANE BOOKS

Published by
**Sandy Lane Books**
Sandy Lane West, Oxford, England
ISBN 0 7459 4010 2
**Albatross Books Pty Ltd**
ISBN 0 7324 1343 5

First edition 1984
This edition 1995
10 9 8 7 6 5 4 3 2 1 0

**Acknowledgments**
Bible quotations, by permission of the copyright holders: Good News Bible, copyright 1966, 1971 and 1976 American Bible Society; published by Bible Societies/Collins

Photographs by Sonia Halliday and Laura Lushington, apart from the following:
Sonia Halliday Photographs/F.H.C. Birch, pages 11, 45; /Sister Daniel, pages 70–71; /Pru Grice, pages 14–15; /Barry Searle, pages 10, 33, 42; /Jane Taylor, pages 16–17, 78–79
British Museum, pages 36–37
Lion Publishing/David Alexander, pages 18–19, 40–41

A catalogue record for this title is available from the British Library

Printed and bound in Singapore

# Contents

I have chosen him to serve me,
to make my name known to Gentiles
and kings and to the people of Israel.
And I myself will show him all that
he must suffer for my sake.

Words of Jesus, from Acts 9

# PART ONE
## PAUL, THE TRAVELLER

# 'A Jew, Born in Tarsus'

*Almost 2,000 years ago a man called Paul, under arrest and facing a screaming mob, stood on the garrison steps in Jerusalem to speak in his own defence. He began with these words, 'I am a Jew, born in Tarsus ...' Because a doctor called Luke set down a careful record of Paul's dramatic conversion and his eventful life, and because thirteen of Paul's own letters still survive, we can meet this remarkable man today in the pages of the Bible.*

*Paul's world – the world of the first century AD, dominated by the power of Rome and Greek culture, pagan, superstitious – and our world have much in common. Certainly both share the same deep need for the Good News Paul brought of new life made possible through Jesus Christ, for hope to lift men and women from despair.*
*As Paul brought his message to Jews and non-Jews, to Athens and Corinth and Rome itself, some made an instant response. Others were violent in their opposition.*
*Who then was this man? A Jew of Jews with a mission also to non-Jews. A free-born Roman citizen. God's man for his time. But let him speak for himself ...*

I am a Jew, born in Tarsus in Cilicia, but brought up here in Jerusalem as a student of Gamaliel.

I received strict instruction in the Law of our ancestors.
Acts 22

I was circumcised when I was a week old. I am an Israelite by birth, of the tribe of Benjamin, a pure-blooded Hebrew.

As far as keeping the Law is concerned I was a Pharisee.
Letter to the Philippians, 3

*Traffic rattles through the ancient gateway of Tarsus, the city where Paul was born.*

# WITH MURDER IN MIND

*To Paul (Saul is his Jewish name), totally dedicated to God, committed from his earliest years to keeping the Jewish Law down to its finest detail, the followers of Jesus were blasphemous heretics.*

*Two or three years earlier the Jewish religious leaders believed they had dealt with the troublesome Galilean once and for all. Jesus was put to death by crucifixion.*

*Just three days later his followers claimed to have seen him, alive again. God had raised him from the dead!*

*Within six weeks they were publicly declaring that 'this Jesus, whom you crucified, is the one that God has made Lord and Messiah!' Thousands responded to the apostles' appeal to 'be baptized in the name of Jesus Christ, so that your sins will be forgiven; and you will receive God's gift, the Holy Spirit'.*

*Now, the Jewish council had received a report that one of Jesus' followers, a man called Stephen, was saying, 'Jesus of Nazareth will tear down the Temple and change all the customs which have come down to us from Moses'. The charge was false, but Paul was filled with cold fury.*

*Stephen was called to account ...*

As the members of the Council listened to Stephen, they became furious and ground their teeth at him in anger. But Stephen, full of the Holy Spirit, looked up to heaven and saw God's glory and Jesus standing at the right-hand side of God.

'Look!' he said. 'I see heaven opened and the Son of Man standing at the right-hand side of God!'

## Paul's own admission

**I myself thought that I should do everything I could against the cause of Jesus of Nazareth. That is what I did in Jerusalem. I received authority from the chief priests and put many of God's people in prison; and when they were sentenced to death, I also voted against them. Many times I had them punished in the synagogues and tried to make them deny their faith. I was so furious with them that I even went to foreign cities to persecute them.**

Acts 27

With a loud cry the members of the Council covered their ears with their hands. Then they all rushed at him at once, threw him out of the city, and stoned him.

The witnesses left their cloaks in the care of a young man named Saul.

They kept on stoning Stephen as he called out to the Lord, 'Lord Jesus, receive my spirit!' He knelt down and cried out in a loud voice, 'Lord! Do not remember this sin against them!' He said this and died.

And Saul approved of his murder.

That very day the church in Jerusalem began to suffer cruel persecution. All the believers, except the apostles, were scattered throughout the provinces of Judaea and Samaria. Some devout men buried Stephen, mourning for him with loud cries. But Saul tried to destroy the church; going from house to house, he dragged out the believers, both men and women, and threw them into jail...

Saul kept up his violent threats of murder against the followers of the Lord. He went to the High Priest and asked for letters of introduction to the synagogues in Damascus, so that if he should find there any followers of the Way of the Lord, he would be able to arrest them, both men and women, and bring them back to Jerusalem.

Acts 7 – 9

*It was in Jerusalem that Stephen died and Paul began his violent persecution of the followers of Jesus.*

# Paul Meets Jesus

*Paul was on his way to Damascus, the Syrian capital, with murder in his heart, when events took a turn he could never have imagined in his wildest dreams.*

As Saul was coming near the city of Damascus, suddenly a light from the sky flashed round him. He fell to the ground and heard a voice saying to him, 'Saul, Saul! Why do you persecute me?'

'Who are you, Lord?' he asked.

'I am Jesus, whom you persecute,' the voice said. 'But get up and go into the city, where you will be told what you must do.'

The men who were travelling with Saul had stopped, not saying a word; they heard the voice but could not see anyone. Saul got up from the ground and opened his eyes, but could not see a thing. So they took him by the hand and led him into Damascus. For three days he was not able to see and during that time he did not eat or drink anything.

There was a Christian in Damascus named Ananias. He had a vision in which the Lord said to him, 'Ananias!'

'Here I am, Lord,' he answered.

The Lord said to him, 'Get ready and go to

Straight Street, and at the house of Judas ask for a man from Tarsus named Saul. He is praying, and in a vision he has seen a man named Ananias come in and place his hands on him so that he might see again.'

Ananias answered, 'Lord, many people have told me about this man and about all the terrible things he has done to your people in Jerusalem. And he has come to Damascus with authority from the chief priests to arrest all who worship you.'

The Lord said to him, 'Go, because I have chosen him to serve me, to make my name known to Gentiles and kings and to the people of Israel. And I myself will show him all that he must suffer for my sake.'

So Ananias went, entered the house where Saul was, and placed his hands on him. 'Brother Saul,' he said, 'the Lord has sent me – Jesus himself, who appeared to you on the road as you were coming here. He sent me so that you might see again and be filled with the Holy Spirit.'

At once something like fish scales fell from Saul's eyes, and he was able to see again. He stood up and was baptized; and after he had eaten, his strength came back.

Acts 9

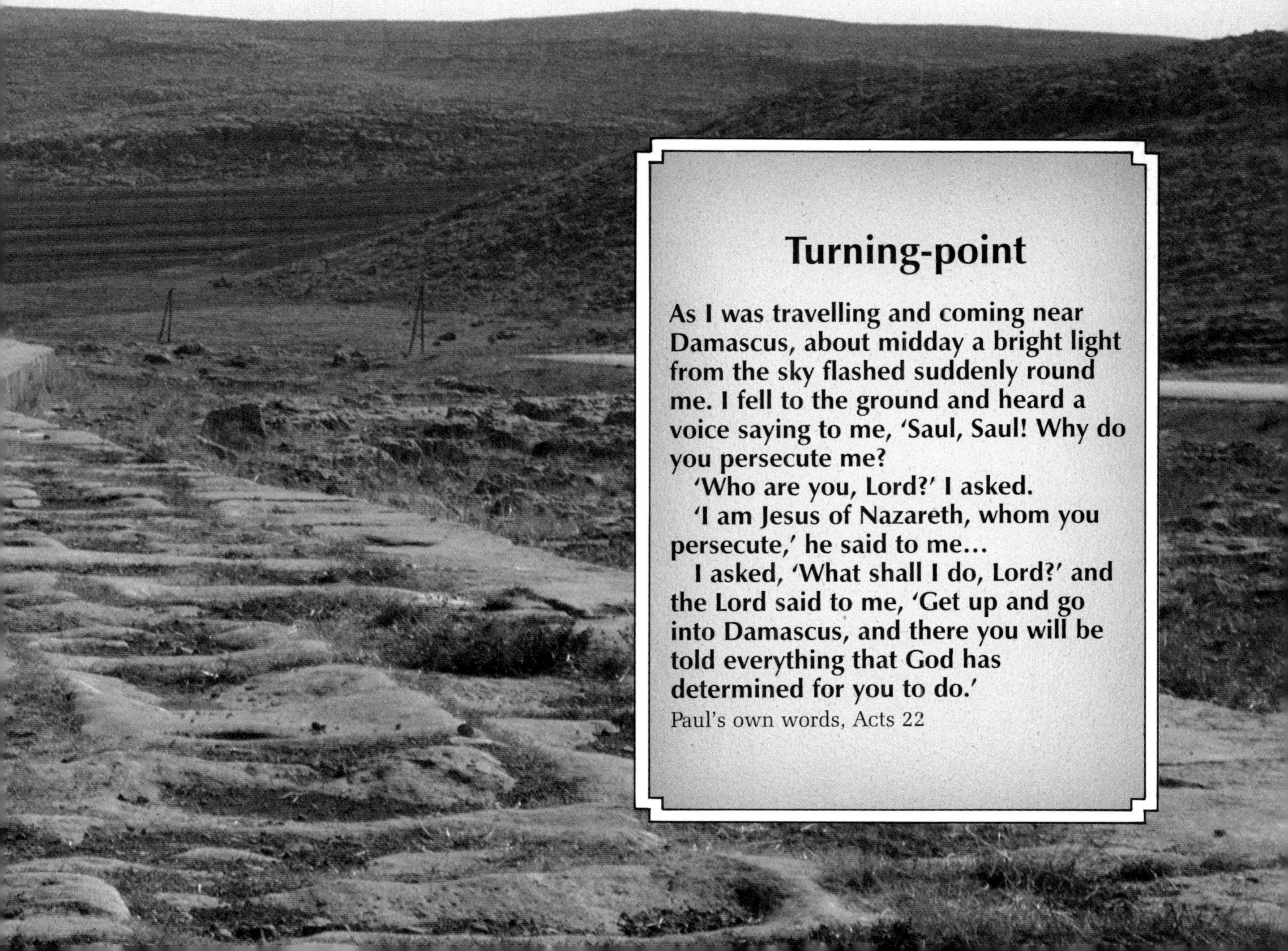

## Turning-point

**As I was travelling and coming near Damascus, about midday a bright light from the sky flashed suddenly round me. I fell to the ground and heard a voice saying to me, 'Saul, Saul! Why do you persecute me?**

**'Who are you, Lord?' I asked.**

**'I am Jesus of Nazareth, whom you persecute,' he said to me...**

**I asked, 'What shall I do, Lord?' and the Lord said to me, 'Get up and go into Damascus, and there you will be told everything that God has determined for you to do.'**

Paul's own words, Acts 22

# Time Out: the Silent Years

*The meeting with Jesus turned Paul's life inside-out and upside-down. The energy and conviction which up to this point had been turned against the followers of Jesus in bitter persecution now had a new focus and direction. Paul went straight to the Jews in the city, who were expecting his arrival, and declared his new-found faith in Jesus as the Messiah, God's long-promised Saviour.*

*But he needed time to think through all that had happened and what it meant. So he took time out in 'Arabia', alone with God.*

*When he returned to Damascus he was soon in trouble for his outspoken teaching. He escaped in undignified fashion, let down from the city walls in a basket one dark night. From there he went to Jerusalem, 'preaching boldly in the name of the Lord'. When they discovered that his life was in danger, his fellow-believers took him to Caesarea, put him on a ship and sent him home to Tarsus.*

**Apostle of Jesus Christ**

Let me tell you, my brothers, that the gospel I preach is not of human origin. I did not receive it from any man, nor did anyone

teach it to me. It was Jesus Christ himself who revealed it to me …

When God decided to reveal his Son to me, so that I might preach the Good News about him to the Gentiles, I did not go to anyone for advice, nor did I go to Jerusalem to see those who were apostles before me. Instead, I went at once to Arabia, and then I returned to Damascus. It was three years later that I went to Jerusalem to obtain information from Peter, and I stayed with him for two weeks. I did not see any other apostle except James, the Lord's brother …

Afterwards I went to places in Syria and Cilicia. At that time the members of the churches in Judaea did not know me personally. They knew only what others were saying: 'The man who used to persecute us is now preaching the faith that he once tried to destroy!' And so they praised God because of me.

Paul's words, from the Letter to Galatians, 1

*Time away from the crowded city, in 'Arabia' gave Paul the opportunity to think through his new-found faith.*

# 'Come and Help Us'

*The New Testament is silent about the years that followed Paul's return to Tarsus.*
*For eleven years he remained in the province around his home.*
*Tarsus on the Cilician plain, the south coast of modern Turkey, was an important city. It had its own university and a population of 500,000 people. It was a meeting-place of East and West.*
*We can only speculate on the reaction of Paul's proud and respectable Jewish family to his new-found faith. He was not one to keep quiet about it, so it is likely these years were hard. 'For Christ's sake,' Paul was to say later, 'I did in actual fact suffer the loss of everything' –*
*every advantage he had by birth. In the years back home Paul learned endurance as God prepared him – in middle age – for the next great change in his life.*

Some of the believers who were scattered by the persecution which took place when Stephen was killed went as far as Phoenicia, Cyprus, and Antioch, telling the message to Jews only. But other believers, men from Cyprus and Cyrene, went to Antioch and proclaimed the message to Gentiles also, telling them the Good News about the Lord Jesus. The Lord's power was with them, and a great number of people believed and turned to the Lord.

The news about this reached the church in Jerusalem, so they sent Barnabas to Antioch. When he arrived and saw how God had blessed the people, he was glad and urged them all to be faithful and true to the Lord with all their hearts. Barnabas was a good man, full of the Holy Spirit and faith, and many people were brought to the Lord.

Then Barnabas went to Tarsus to look for

Saul. When he found him, he took him to Antioch, and for a whole year the two met with the people of the church and taught a large group. It was at Antioch that the believers were first called Christians ...

In the church at Antioch there were some prophets and teachers: Barnabas, Simeon (called the Black), Lucius (from Cyrene), Manaen (who had been brought up with Herod the governor), and Saul. While they were serving the Lord and fasting, the Holy Spirit said to them, 'Set apart for me Barnabas and Saul, to do the work to which I have called them.'

They fasted and prayed, placed their hands on them, and sent them off.

Acts 12 and 13

## Chosen to serve

**God in his grace chose me even before I was born, and called me to serve him.**

Paul's words, from the Letter to the Galatians, 1

*Antioch in Syria, where the followers of Jesus were first nicknamed 'Christians', is still today a bustling city on the River Orontes. In Paul's day it had its own sea-port and was capital of the Roman province of Syria, third largest city of the Roman Empire.*

# 'A Light for the Gentiles'

*Paul and Barnabas, with his young cousin John Mark (who gave his name to the second Gospel), set off by sea for Cyprus, Barnabas' birth-place. After a dramatic encounter with the island's governor and the magician Elymas at Paphos they continued their journey, crossing to mainland Turkey. At Perga John Mark left them – a desertion Paul found it hard to forgive.*

*Several days' journey over rough mountain tracks brought them to Antioch in Pisidia. At the Jewish synagogue on the Sabbath, after the usual readings, Paul was invited to speak. He stood up to address his fellow-Jews 'and all Gentiles here who worship God'.*

*He soon came to the point …*

'We want you to know, my fellow-Israelites, that it is through Jesus that the message about forgiveness of sins is preached to you; and that everyone who believes in him is set free from all the sins from which the Law of Moses could not set you free. Take care, then, so that what the prophets said may not happen to you:

' "Look, you scoffers! Be astonished and die!
For what I am doing today
is something that you will not believe,
even when someone explains it to you!" '

As Paul and Barnabas were leaving the synagogue, the people invited them to come back the next Sabbath and tell them more about these things. After the people had left the meeting, Paul and Barnabas were followed by many Jews and by many Gentiles who had been converted to Judaism. The apostles spoke to them and encouraged them to keep on living in the grace of God.

The next Sabbath nearly everyone in the town came to hear the word of the Lord. When the Jews saw the crowds, they were filled with jealousy; they disputed what Paul was saying and insulted him. But Paul and Barnabas spoke out even more boldly:

'It was necessary that the word of God should be spoken first to you. But since you reject it and do not consider yourselves worthy of eternal life, we will leave you and go to the Gentiles. For this is the commandment that the Lord has given us:
' "I have made you a light for the Gentiles,
so that all the world may be saved." '

When the Gentiles heard this, they were glad and praised the Lord's message; and those who had been chosen for eternal life became believers.

The word of the Lord spread everywhere in that region. But the Jews stirred up the leading men of the city and the Gentile women of high social standing who worshipped God. They started a persecution against Paul and Barnabas and threw them out of their region. The apostles shook the dust off their feet in protest against them and went on to Iconium.

Acts 13

*Paul and his friends travelled by sea as well as by land to take the Good News of Jesus to Cyprus, Turkey and Greece. He actually used the port pictured here – Neapolis (Kavalla) in northern Greece.*

# A Bull for Zeus

*Time and again the pattern was repeated. Paul and Barnabas, arriving at a new town, spoke first to the Jews and God-fearing Gentiles at the synagogue. They met with a mixed response. Some welcomed the Good News with joy. But sooner or later the traditionalists amongst the Jews stirred up trouble. Having discharged their responsibility to their fellow-Jews, Paul and Barnabas then turned to the eager Gentiles. It was not without deep personal regret, as Paul's Letter to the Romans reveals. But they were doing as God instructed.*

*The events at Antioch were repeated at Iconium, where the apostles narrowly escaped stoning. They fled to the cities of Lystra and Derbe to preach the Good News – and to meet with a surprising reaction from the pagan crowd.*

In Lystra there was a man who had been lame from birth and had never been able to walk. He sat there and listened to Paul's words. Paul saw that he believed and could be healed, so he looked straight at him and said in a loud voice, 'Stand up straight on your feet!' The man jumped up and started walking around.

When the crowds saw what Paul had done, they started shouting in their own Lycaonian language, 'The gods have become like men and have come down to us!' They gave Barnabas the name Zeus, and Paul the name Hermes, because he was the chief speaker. The priest of the god Zeus, whose temple stood just outside the town, brought bulls and flowers to the gate, for he and the crowds wanted to offer sacrifice to the apostles.

When Barnabas and Paul heard what they were about to do, they tore their clothes and ran into the middle of the crowd, shouting, 'Why are you doing this? We ourselves are only human beings like you! We are here to announce the Good News, to turn you away from these worthless things to the living God, who made heaven, earth, sea, and all that is in them. In the past he allowed all people to go their own way. But he has always given evidence of his existence by the good things he does: he gives you rain from heaven and crops at the right times; he gives you food and fills your hearts with happiness.' Even with these words the apostles could hardly keep the crowd from offering a sacrifice to them.
Acts 14

*At Lystra the priest of Zeus brought bulls and garlands to honour Paul and Barnabas as gods. Paganism may have been bankrupt: it was certainly not dead. It provided both opposition and opportunity for the new faith.*

# Charter of Freedom

*Jews from Antioch and Iconium followed Paul to Lystra. He was stoned and left for dead. But he recovered consciousness and he and Barnabas went on to Derbe. With incredible courage they made their way back to the coast and a ship home, passing through each of the towns of the outward journey. In every church they appointed leaders, encouraging the new Christians and warning them that 'we must pass through many troubles to enter the Kingdom of God'. Home in Syrian Antioch they gave a full report to the church of all that God had done 'and how he had opened the way for the Gentiles to believe'. At last there was rest, and the company of friends. But only for a time. The issues raised by those who insisted that Gentile believers must be circumcised and obey the Law of Moses had to be resolved. It took a full-scale Council to establish the charter of freedom …*

Some men came from Judaea to Antioch and started teaching the believers, 'You cannot be saved unless you are circumcised as the Law of Moses requires.'

Paul and Barnabas got into a fierce argument with them about this, so it was decided that Paul and Barnabas and some of the others in Antioch should go to Jerusalem and see the apostles and elders about this matter …

When they arrived in Jerusalem, they were welcomed by the church, the apostles, and the elders, to whom they told all that God had done through them. But some of the believers who belonged to the party of the Pharisees stood up and said, 'The Gentiles must be circumcised and told to obey the Law of Moses.'

The apostles and the elders met together to consider this question. After a long debate Peter stood up and said, 'My brothers, you know that a long time ago God chose me from among you to preach the Good News to the Gentiles, so that they could hear and believe. And God, who knows the thoughts of everyone, showed his approval of the Gentiles by giving the Holy Spirit to them, just as he had to us. He made no difference between us and them; he forgave their sins because they believed. So then, why do you now want to put God to the test by laying a load on the

backs of the believers which neither our ancestors nor we ourselves were able to carry? No! We believe and are saved by the grace of the Lord Jesus, just as they are.'

The whole group was silent as they heard Barnabas and Paul report all the miracles and wonders that God had performed through them among the Gentiles.

When they had finished speaking, James spoke up: 'Listen to me, my brothers! Simon has just explained how God first showed his care for the Gentiles by taking from among them a people to belong to him. The words of the prophets agree completely with this ...

'It is my opinion,' James went on, 'that we should not trouble the Gentiles who are turning to God. Instead, we should write a letter telling them not to eat any food that is ritually unclean because it has been offered to idols; to keep themselves from sexual immorality; and not to eat any animal that has been strangled, or any blood. For the Law of Moses has been read for a very long time in the synagogues every Sabbath, and his words are preached in every town ...'

The messengers were sent off and went to Antioch, where they gathered the whole group of believers and gave them the letter. When the people read it, they were filled with joy by the message of encouragement.

Acts 15

*Jerusalem, where the church began, was the setting for the first great council. The question was, should non-Jewish Christians be circumcised and required to keep the Jewish Law. No! Jew and Gentile alike are saved simply by faith in Christ. Nothing need be added.*

# PAUL – AND FRIENDS

*Barnabas suggested taking Mark with them on a new mission. But Paul still felt so sore about Mark's earlier desertion that there was a bitter argument. It ended with the two men going their separate ways. Barnabas sailed for Cyprus with Mark (who from this point on proved totally loyal and dependable).*

*Paul made his way overland to visit the churches established on the first journey. His chosen companion was Silas, a leader of the Jerusalem church.*

*In the course of their travels Paul and Silas were joined first by Timothy, then by Luke, who recorded their journeys in his book of Acts. These three friends, with another non-Jewish Christian called Titus, became Paul's constant companions and an enormous support, not only to the apostle himself but also to the young and growing churches.*

*In his letters Paul mentions these friends often, with deep affection and thankfulness. Timothy, in particular, was the son Paul never had, sensitive and diffident but utterly loyal and true.*

**A new companion**

Paul travelled on to Derbe and Lystra, where a Christian named Timothy lived. His mother, who was also a Christian, was Jewish, but his father was a Greek. All the believers in Lystra and Iconium spoke well of Timothy. Paul wanted to take Timothy along with him, so he circumcised him. He did so because all the Jews who lived in those places knew that Timothy's father was Greek. As they went through the towns, they delivered to the believers the rules decided upon by the apostles and elders in Jerusalem and told them to obey those rules. So the churches were made stronger in the faith and grew in numbers every day.

Acts 16

**Testimonial – from Paul to Timothy**

I give thanks to God, whom I serve with a clear conscience, as my ancestors did. I thank him as I remember you always in my prayers night and day. I remember your tears, and I want to see you very much, so that I may be filled with joy. I remember the sincere faith you have, the kind of faith that your grandmother Lois and your mother Eunice also had. I am sure that you have it also. For this reason I remind you to keep alive the gift that God gave you when I laid my hands on you. For the Spirit that God has given us does not make us timid; instead, his Spirit fills us with power, love, and self-control.

Second Letter to Timothy, 1 and 2

**A word of advice**

My son, be strong through the grace that is ours in union with Christ Jesus. Take the teachings that you heard me proclaim in the presence of many witnesses, and entrust them to reliable people, who will be able to teach others also.

Take your part in suffering, as a loyal soldier of Christ Jesus …

Continue in the truths that you were taught and firmly believe. You know who your teachers were, and you remember that ever since you were a child, you have known the Holy Scriptures, which are able to give you the wisdom that leads to salvation through faith in Christ Jesus. All Scripture is inspired by God and is useful for teaching the truth, rebuking error, correcting faults, and giving instruction for right living, so that the person who serves God may be fully qualified and equipped to do every kind of good deed.

Second Letter to Timothy, 3

*Paul did not travel alone. He took with him young men from the local churches to share in the work of spreading the gospel. This was helped by the fact that everywhere they went there were great Hellenistic cities sharing a common culture and civilization. Even more important, they shared a common language, everyday (koine) Greek. This was the language in which the New Testament was written.*

## Take courage

**This is a true saying:**
**If we have died with him,**
**we shall also live with him.**
**If we continue to endure,**
**we shall also rule with him.**
**If we deny him,**
**he also will deny us.**
**If we are not faithful,**
**he remains faithful,**
**because he cannot be false to himself.**
Second Letter to Timothy, 2

# 'We are Roman Citizens'

*Paul was being questioned by a Roman officer.*
*'Are you a Roman citizen?' he asked.*
*'Yes,' answered Paul.*
*'I became one by paying a large sum of money,' the soldier said.*
*'But I am one by birth,' Paul replied.*
*In a world dominated by Roman power Paul was in a privileged position, one the soldier envied.*

*Paul and his friends left Lystra intending to travel further inland. But God blocked the way. They were at Troas, on the west coast of Turkey, when Paul had a vision. A man from northern Greece, just across the sea, was calling to him. So they set sail – and brought the Good News across the Aegean to Europe. At the Roman colony of Philippi, their first stop inland, they were welcomed into the home of a businesswoman called Lydia, who responded gladly to their teaching. They stayed some time. Then there was trouble when Paul exorcised a slave-girl. The authorities were quick to act. Paul and Silas were summarily flogged and flung into jail, no questions asked …*

The jailer threw them into the inner cell and fastened their feet between heavy blocks of wood.

About midnight Paul and Silas were praying and singing hymns to God, and the other prisoners were listening to them. Suddenly there was a violent earthquake, which shook the prison to its foundations. At once all the doors opened, and the chains fell off all the prisoners.

The jailer woke up, and when he saw the prison doors open, he thought that the prisoners had escaped; so he pulled out his sword and was about to kill himself. But Paul shouted at the top of his voice.

'Don't harm yourself! We are all here!'

The jailer called for a light, rushed in, and fell trembling at the feet of Paul and Silas. Then he led them out and asked, 'Sirs, what must I do to be saved?'

They answered, 'Believe in the Lord Jesus, and you will be saved – you and your family.'

Then they preached the word of the Lord to him and to all the others in his house. At that very hour of the night the jailer took them and washed their wounds; and he and all his family were baptized at once. Then he took Paul and Silas up into his house and gave them some food to eat. He and his family were filled with joy, because they now believed in God.

The next morning the Roman authorities sent police officers with the order, 'Let those men go.'

So the jailer told Paul, 'The officials have sent an order for you and Silas to be released. You may leave, then, and go in peace.'

But Paul said to the police officers, 'We were not found guilty of any crime, yet they whipped us in public – and we are Roman citizens! Then they threw us in prison. And now they want to send us away secretly. Not likely! The Roman officials themselves must come here and let us out.'

The police officers reported these words to the Roman officials; and when they heard that Paul and Silas were Roman citizens, they were afraid. So they went and apologized to them; then they led them out of the prison and asked them to leave the city.

Paul and Silas left the prison and went to Lydia's house. There they met the believers, spoke words of encouragement to them, and left.

Acts 16

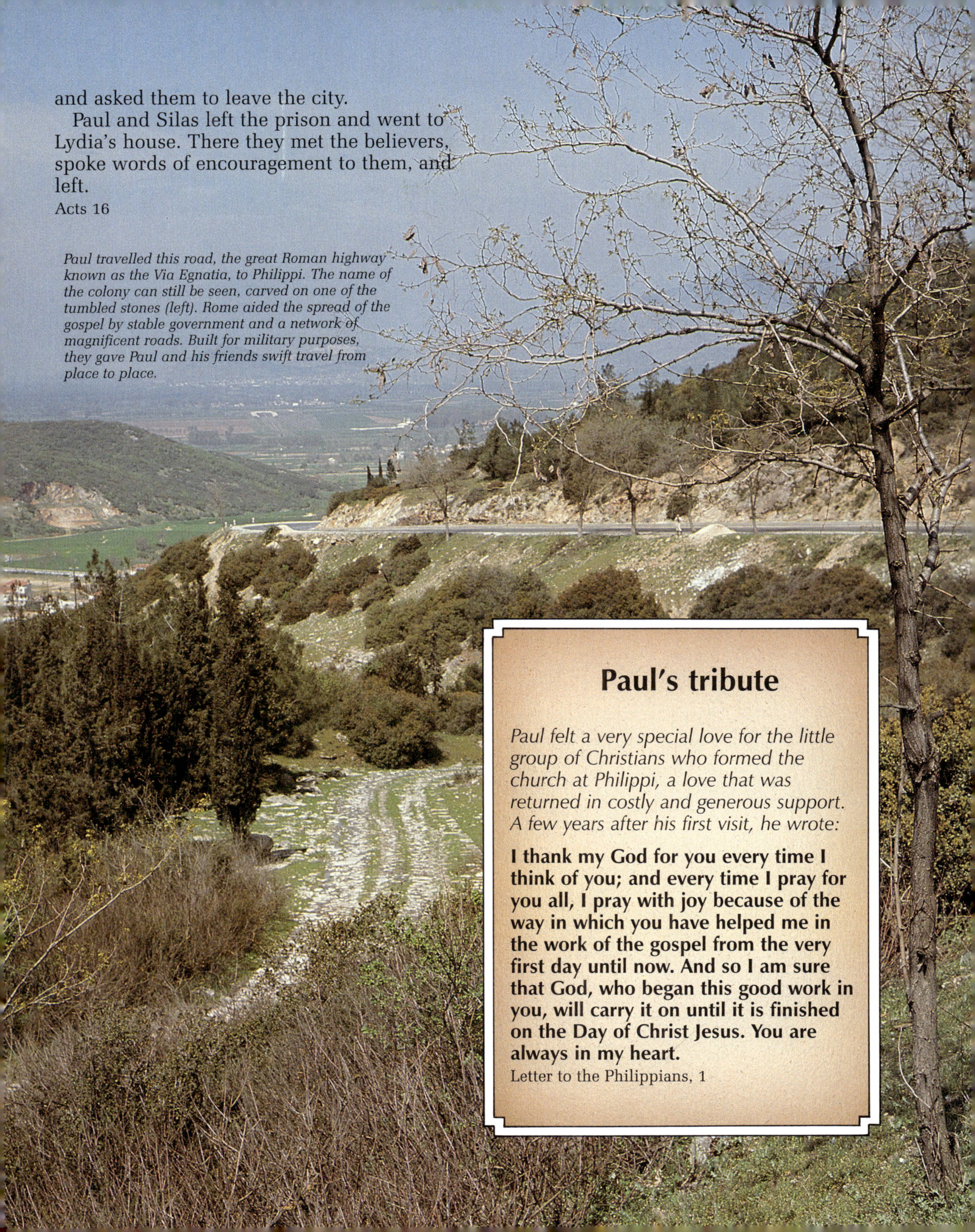

*Paul travelled this road, the great Roman highway known as the Via Egnatia, to Philippi. The name of the colony can still be seen, carved on one of the tumbled stones (left). Rome aided the spread of the gospel by stable government and a network of magnificent roads. Built for military purposes, they gave Paul and his friends swift travel from place to place.*

## Paul's tribute

*Paul felt a very special love for the little group of Christians who formed the church at Philippi, a love that was returned in costly and generous support. A few years after his first visit, he wrote:*

**I thank my God for you every time I think of you; and every time I pray for you all, I pray with joy because of the way in which you have helped me in the work of the gospel from the very first day until now. And so I am sure that God, who began this good work in you, will carry it on until it is finished on the Day of Christ Jesus. You are always in my heart.**

Letter to the Philippians, 1

# God the Creator

*From Philippi Paul and Silas travelled the famous trade-route known as the Egnatian Way to Thessalonika, a bustling city and hub of northern Greece. There it was the same story as before: preaching, mixed response, trouble. But a church was planted which, as Paul's two letters to the Thessalonian Christians show, brought him lasting satisfaction.*

*At nearby Berea there was a more positive response. Paul's hearers eagerly 'searched the Scriptures' to see if what he said was really true. As a result, many believed.*

*But troublemakers came from Thessalonika. Paul was sent on, leaving Silas and Timothy to build up the work and join him later.*

*So Paul came to Athens, the greatest city in all Greece, a city glorying in its past, justly proud of its culture and intellect, whose people delighted in philosophical debate and were ready to give any new ideas a hearing.*

While Paul was waiting in Athens for Silas and Timothy, he was greatly upset when he noticed how full of idols the city was.

So he held discussions in the synagogue with the Jews and with the Gentiles who worshipped God, and also in the public square every day with the people who happened to pass by.

Certain Epicurean and Stoic teachers also debated with him. Some of them asked, 'What is this ignorant show-off trying to say?'

Others answered, 'He seems to be talking about foreign gods.' They said this because Paul was preaching about Jesus and the resurrection.

So they took Paul, brought him before the city council, the Areopagus, and said, 'We would like to know what this new teaching is that you are talking about. Some of the things we hear you say sound strange to us, and we would like to know what they mean.' (For all

the citizens of Athens and the foreigners who lived there liked to spend all their time telling and hearing the latest new thing.)

Paul stood up in front of the city council and said, 'I see that in every way you Athenians are very religious. For as I walked through your city and looked at the places where you worship, I found an altar on which is written "To an Unknown God". That which you worship, then, even though you do not know it, is what I now proclaim to you.

'God, who made the world and everything in it, is Lord of heaven and earth and does not live in mad-made temples. Nor does he need anything that we can supply by working for him, since it is he himself who gives life and breath and everything else to everyone.

'From one man he created all races of mankind and made them live throughout the whole earth. He himself fixed beforehand the exact times and the limits of the places where they would live. He did this so that they would look for him, and perhaps find him as they felt about for him.

'Yet God is actually not far from any one of us; as someone has said,

"In him we live and move and exist."

It is as some of your poets have said,

"We too are his children."

'Since we are God's children, we should not suppose that his nature is anything like an image of gold or silver or stone, shaped by the art and skill of man. God has overlooked the times when people did not know him, but now he commands all of them everywhere to turn away from their evil ways. For he has fixed a day in which he will judge the whole world with justice by means of a man he has chosen. He has given proof of this to everyone by raising that man from death!'

Acts 17

*Paul's method of making the new faith known was to start with the strategic cities. From these centres the news spread far and wide. Athens, the greatest city in all Greece, was an obvious target.*

# City of Love

*From Athens Paul crossed the narrow neck of land which separates the Aegean and Adriatic seas, to reach Corinth. It was a city with a bad reputation, dominated by the temple of Aphrodite, goddess of love, with its thousands of temple prostitutes.*
*A city so strategically placed for trade was bound to attract a large floating population. Corinth was a racial hotch-potch, a place where 'anything goes'.*
*It was a tough environment in which to preach the gospel of a very different kind of love. Yet Paul, like the city's merchants, could see the potential. From Corinth the Good News could spread far and wide.*
*Paul made his home with a Jewish couple, Aquila and Priscilla, newly arrived from Italy. All three earned a living from tent-making. And the seeds of the gospel were sown …*

When Silas and Timothy arrived from Macedonia, Paul gave his whole time to preaching the message, testifying to the Jews that Jesus is the Messiah. When they opposed him and said evil things about him, he protested by shaking the dust from his clothes and saying to them,

'If you are lost, you yourselves must take the blame for it! I am not responsible. From now on I will go to the Gentiles.'

So he left them and went to live in the house of a Gentile named Titius Justus, who worshipped God; his house was next to the synagogue.

Crispus, who was the leader of the synagogue, believed in the Lord, together with all his family; and many other people in Corinth heard the message, believed, and were baptized.

One night Paul had a vision in which the Lord said to him, 'Do not be afraid, but keep on speaking and do not give up, for I am with you. No one will be able to harm you, for many in this city are my people.'

So Paul stayed there for a year and a half, teaching the people the word of God.

**An important ruling**

When Gallio was made the Roman governor of Achaia, the Jews got together, seized Paul, and took him into court.

'This man,' they said, 'is trying to persuade people to worship God in a way that is against the law!'

Paul was about to speak when Gallio said to the Jews, 'If this were a matter of some evil crime or wrong that has been committed, it would be reasonable for me to be patient with you Jews. But since it is an argument about words and names and your own law, you yourselves must settle it. I will not be the judge of such things!' And he drove them out of the court.

Acts 18

*Corinth, another great city in southern Greece, was a centre of trade. Here, where races and nations mixed, Paul saw the birth of a new church.*

## True Love

*Some time after his visit Paul wrote a letter to the Christians at Corinth. In it he gives this moving description of true love – self-giving, patient, kind – in stark contrast to the self-seeking, self-gratifying love of the world around.*

**I may be able to speak the languages of men and even of angels, but if I have no love, my speech is no more than a noisy gong or a clanging bell.**

**I may have the gift of inspired preaching; I may have all knowledge and understand all secrets; I may have all the faith needed to move mountains – but if I have no love, I am nothing.**

**I may give away everything I have, and even give up my body to be burnt – but if I have no love, this does me no good.**

**Love is patient and kind; it is not jealous or conceited or proud; love is not ill-mannered or selfish or irritable; love does not keep a record of wrongs; love is not happy with evil, but is happy with the truth. Love never gives up; and its faith, hope and patience never fail.**

**Love is eternal.**

First Letter to the Corinthians, 13

# Uproar at Ephesus

*Gallio's verdict at Corinth was an important one. As far as the Roman authorities were concerned Paul and his fellow-Christians were free to spread their faith.*
*Paul stayed on for some time. Then he set sail for home. Aquila and Priscilla went with him as far as Ephesus. Paul landed at Caesarea, called in on the church at Jerusalem, and returned to Antioch.*
*On his next journey he rejoined his friends. Ephesus was a flourishing city on the west coast of Turkey, where East met West. If Corinth was Aphrodite's city – the city of love – Ephesus was the city of Artemis (Diana). Many earned their living making miniature statues of the goddess to sell to the visitors who flocked to her temple – one of the wonders of the ancient world.*
*For three months Paul held discussions in the synagogue. Then there was opposition and he moved out, taking the new Christians with him. Every day for two years he taught in the lecture-hall of Tyrranus, to such effect that those who had practised magic publicly burnt their books, and the trade in idols began to fall off.*

At this time there was serious trouble in Ephesus because of the Way of the Lord. A certain silversmith named Demetrius made silver models of the temple of the goddess Artemis, and his business brought a great deal of profit to the workers. So he called them all together with others whose work was like theirs and said to them,

'Men, you know that our prosperity comes from this work. Now, you can see and hear for yourselves what this fellow Paul is doing. He says that man-made gods are not gods at all, and he has succeeded in convincing many people, both here in Ephesus and in nearly the whole province of Asia. There is the danger, then, that this business of ours will get a bad name. Not only that, but there is also the danger that the temple of the great goddess Artemis will come to mean nothing and that her greatness will be destroyed – the goddess worshipped by everyone in Asia and in all the world!'

As the crowd heard these words, they became furious and started shouting, 'Great is Artemis of Ephesus!'

The uproar spread throughout the whole city. The mob seized Gaius and Aristarchus, two Macedonians who were travelling with Paul, and rushed with them to the theatre ...

At last the town clerk was able to calm the crowd.

'Fellow-Ephesians!' he said. 'Everyone knows that the city of Ephesus is the keeper of the temple of the great Artemis and of the sacred stone that fell down from heaven. Nobody can deny these things. So then, you must calm down and not do anything reckless. You have brought these men here even though they have not robbed temples or said evil things about our goddess ... There is no excuse for all this uproar, and we would not be able to give a good reason for it.'

After saying this, he dismissed the meeting.
Acts 19

*At Ephesus, city of the goddess Artemis (Diana), Paul once again clashed with paganism. Here the gods of Greece and Rome had met and mixed with earlier eastern beliefs in the great mother-goddess. But the teaching of the Christians turned their world upside-down.*

## Armed for the fight

*Later, when Paul wrote his letter to the Christians in and around Ephesus, he prepared them for the inevitable battle with the forces of evil.*

**Put on all the armour that God gives you, so that you will be able to stand up against the Devil's evil tricks. For we are not fighting against human beings but against the wicked spiritual forces in the heavenly world, the rulers, authorities, and cosmic powers of this dark age. So put on God's armour now! Then when the evil day comes, you will be able to resist the enemy's attacks; and after fighting to the end, you will still hold your ground.**

**So stand ready, with truth as a belt tight round your waist, with righteousness as your breast plate, and as your shoes the readiness to announce the Good News of peace.**

**At all times carry faith as a shield; for with it you will be able to put out all the burning arrows shot by the Evil One.**

**And accept salvation as a helmet, and the word of God as the sword which the Spirit gives you.**

Letter to the Ephesians, 6

'With my own hand I write this:
*Greetings from Paul.*
This is the way I sign every
letter: this is how I write.
May the grace of our Lord Jesus
Christ be with you all.'

Second Letter to the Thessalonians

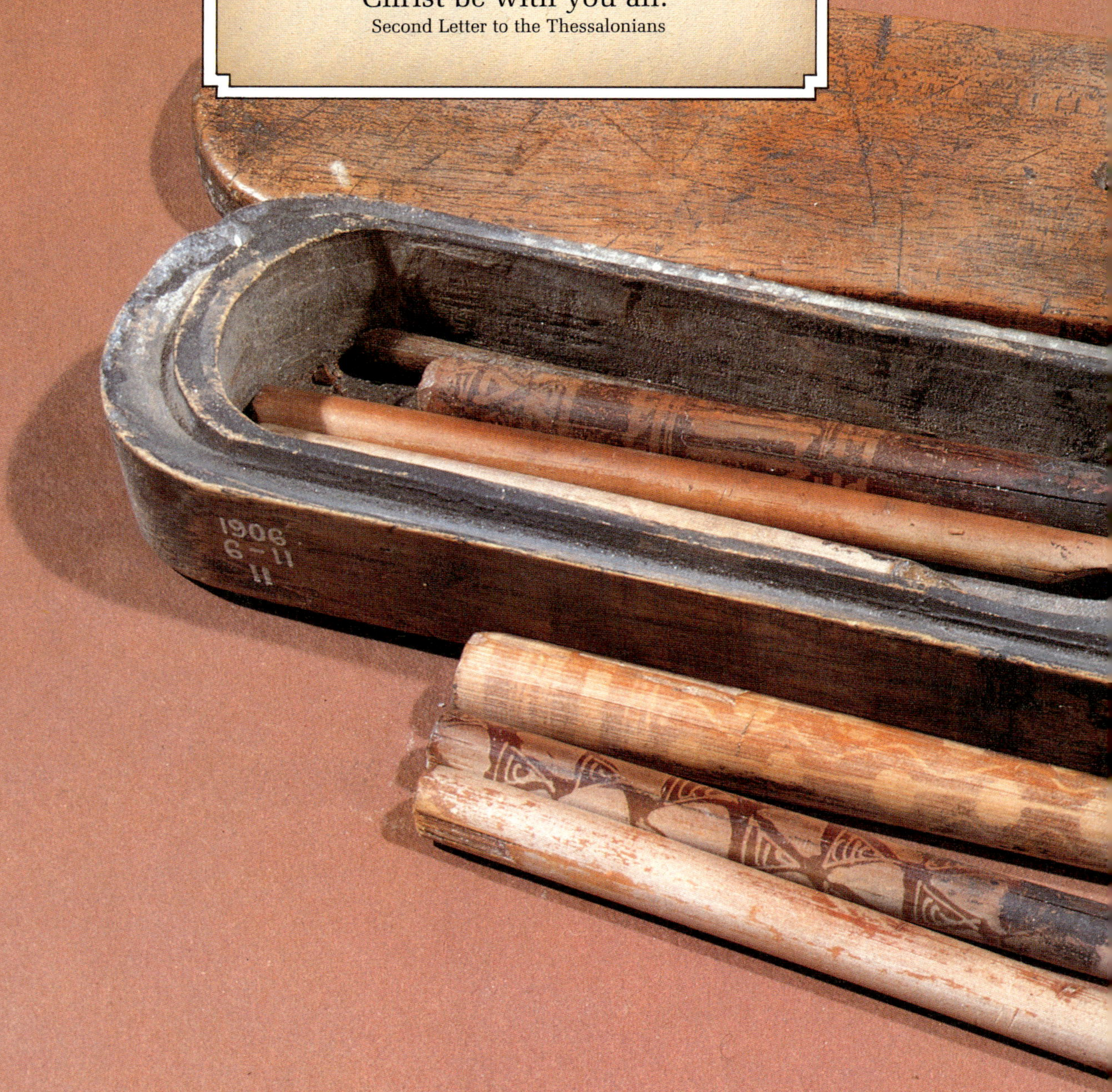

# PART TWO
## Letters from Paul

# Good News for a Lost World

*Paul and his fellow-Christians turned the world of their day upside-down. Lives were changed. Values were challenged, life-styles altered. People found a new purpose in life, new standards, a whole new beginning.*

*What was the secret?*

*It was not in power of personality, or of numbers, or of speech. 'When I came to you,' Paul says, 'I was weak and trembled all over with fear, and my teaching and message were not delivered with skilful words of human wisdom.' No 'big words'. No 'great learning'. The power lay in the message. It was God's message: his Good News for a lost world. And it came with his power – the same incredible power which raised Jesus to life again.*

*New life was God's gift. God's own Spirit was the guarantee to each believer that, day-to-day, they would be able to live for God.*

*What, then, was the message Paul brought to Antioch and Philippi, to Athens and Corinth and Ephesus? To discover this, we need to pause in the 'story' given us by the book of Acts, and turn to the letters which flowed from Paul's pen to the newly-founded churches he cared for so deeply.*

### A lost world

God's anger is revealed from heaven against all the sin and evil of the people whose evil ways prevent the truth from being known. God punishes them, because what can be known about God is plain to them, for God himself made it plain. Ever since God created the world, his invisible qualities, both his eternal power and his divine nature, have been clearly seen; they are perceived in the things that God has made. So those people have no excuse at all! They know God, but they do not give him the honour that belongs to him, nor do they thank him. Instead, their thoughts have become complete nonsense, and their empty minds are filled with darkness. They say they are wise, but they are fools; instead of worshipping the immortal God, they worship images made to look like mortal man or birds or animals or reptiles …

God judges everyone by the same standard. The Gentiles do not have the Law of Moses; they sin and are lost apart from the Law. The Jews have the Law; they sin and are judged by the Law. For it is not by hearing the Law that people are put right with God, but by doing what the Law commands …

Jews and Gentiles alike are all under the power of sin. As the Scriptures say:

'There is no one who is righteous,
no one who is wise
or who worships God.
All have turned away from God;
they have all gone wrong;
no one does what is right, not even one.'

Letter to the Romans, 1 – 3

### The Good News

But now God's way of putting people right with himself has been revealed. It has nothing to do with law, even though the Law of Moses and the prophets gave their witness to it. God puts people right through their faith in Jesus Christ. God does this to all who believe in Christ, because there is no difference at all: everyone has sinned and is far away from God's saving presence. But by the free gift of God's grace all are put right with him through Christ Jesus, who sets them free.

Letter to the Romans, 3

## The power of the Gospel

**I have complete confidence in the gospel; it is God's power to save all who believe, first the Jews and also the Gentiles. For the gospel reveals how God puts people right with himself: it is through faith from beginning to end. As the scripture says, 'The person who is put right with God through faith shall live.'**

Paul's words, Letter to the Romans, 1

*Paul's fullest statement of Christian belief – the message on which he staked his life – was written to the Christians in Rome.*

# The Human Dilemma

*Lost and found! The Good News is that God has stepped into our lost world to put us right with himself. In his letter to the Christians in Rome, whom he longed to see but had not yet visited, Paul spells out the human dilemma in personal terms …*

**Trapped**

Even though the desire to do good is in me, I am not able to do it. I don't do the good I want to do; instead, I do the evil that I do not want to do. If I do what I don't want to do, this means that I am no longer the one who does it; instead, it is the sin that lives in me.

So I find that this law is at work: when I want to do what is good, what is evil is the only choice I have. My inner being delights in the law of God. But I see a different law at work in my body – a law that fights against the law which my mind approves of. It makes me a prisoner to the law of sin which is at work in my body.

What an unhappy man I am! Who will rescue me from this body that is taking me to death?

Thanks be to God, who does this through our Lord Jesus Christ!

This, then is my condition: on my own I can serve God's law only with my mind, while my human nature serves the law of sin.

Letter to the Romans, 7

**Set free**

There is no condemnation now for those who live in union with Christ Jesus. For the law of the Spirit, which brings us life in union with Christ Jesus has set me free from the law of sin and death.

What the Law could not do, because human nature was weak, God did. He condemned sin in human nature by sending his own Son, who came with a nature like man's sinful nature, to do away with sin. God did this so that the righteous demands of the Law might be fully satisfied in us who live according to the Spirit, and not according to human nature.

Those who live as their human nature tells them to, have their minds controlled by what human nature wants. Those who live as the Spirit tells them to, have their minds controlled by what the Spirit wants.

To be controlled by human nature results in death; to be controlled by the Spirit results in life and peace.

Letter to the Romans, 8

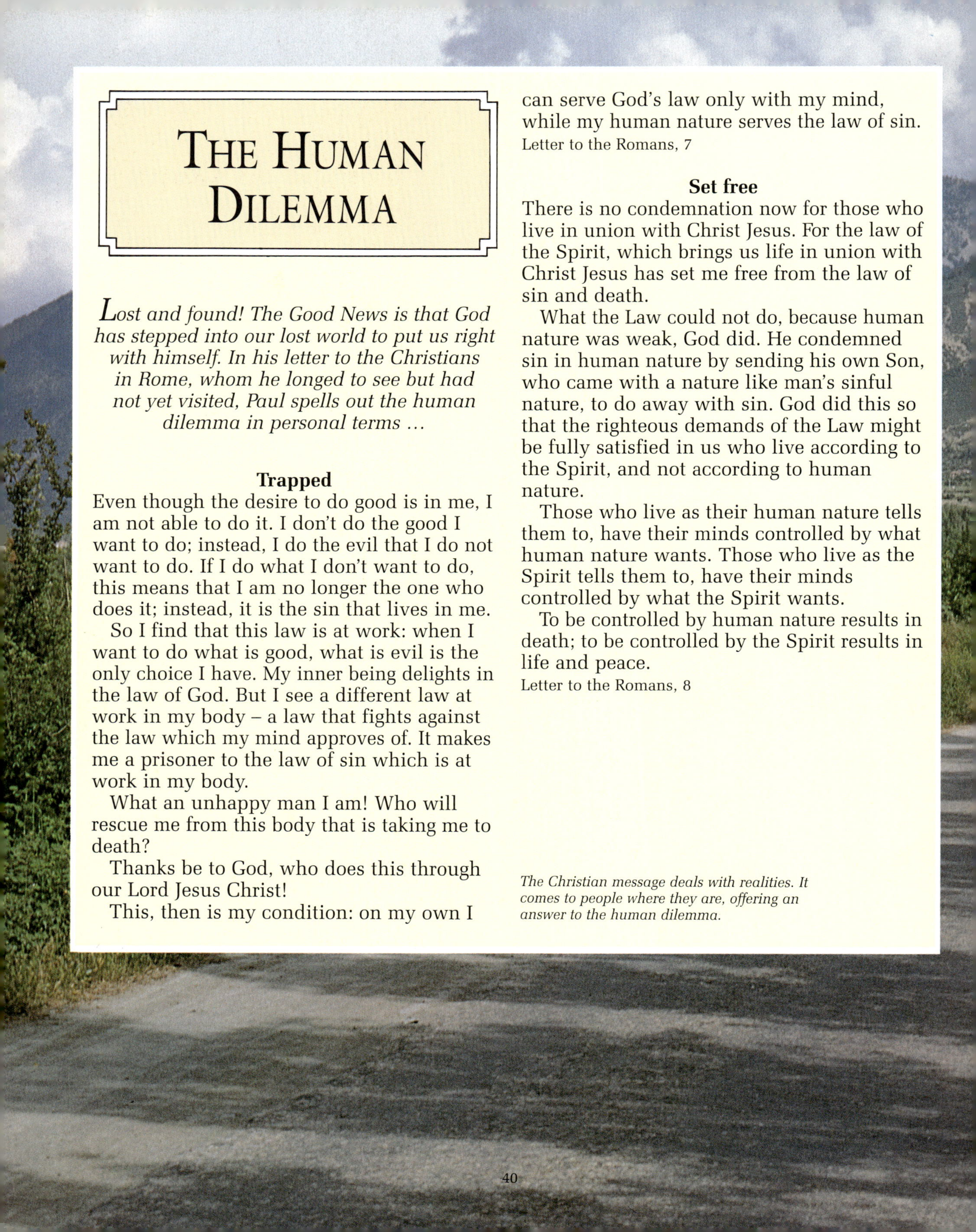

*The Christian message deals with realities. It comes to people where they are, offering an answer to the human dilemma.*

# One Way

*God is offering us life and peace – peace with God; peace with one another. There is only one way we can be brought back to him.*

God's mercy is so abundant, and his love for us is so great, that while we were spiritually dead in our disobedience he brought us to life with Christ. It is by God's grace that you have been saved.

In our union with Christ Jesus he raised us up with him to rule with him in the heavenly world. He did this to demonstrate for all time to come the extraordinary greatness of his grace in the love he showed us in Christ Jesus.

For it is by God's grace that you have been saved through faith. It is not the result of your own efforts, but God's gift, so that no one can boast about it.

God has made us what we are, and in our union with Christ Jesus he has created us for a life of good deeds, which he has already prepared for us to do …

Christ himself has brought us peace by making Jews and Gentiles one people. With his own body he broke down the wall that separated them and kept them enemies. He abolished the Jewish Law with its commandments and rules, in order to create out of the two races one new people in union with himself, in this way making peace. By his death on the cross Christ destroyed their enmity; by means of the cross he united both races into one body and brought them back to God.

So Christ came and preached the Good News of peace to all – to you Gentiles, who were far away from God, and to the Jews, who were near to him. It is through Christ that all of us, Jews and Gentiles, are able to come in the one Spirit into the presence of the Father.

Letter to the Ephesians 2 and 3

*The racial barriers are down. In Christ Jew and non-Jew, black and white, man and woman, are one new people.*

## All are one in Christ

**It is through faith that all of you are God's sons in union with Christ Jesus. You were baptized into union with Christ, and now your are clothed, so to speak, with the life of Christ himself. So there is no difference between Jews and Gentiles, between slaves and free men, between men and women; you are all one in union with Christ Jesus.**

Letter to the Galatians, 3

# Christ Crucified – and Risen

*The death of Jesus for our forgiveness, and his resurrection, were right at the heart of Paul's message.*
*Writing to the Christians in Corinth he said he had determined to forget* everything *but Christ and his death on the cross.*
*At Athens Paul spoke so often of 'Christ' and 'resurrection' that his hearers got confused and thought he was talking about* two *new gods.*

**Christ's death on the cross**

God sent me to tell the Good News, and to tell it without using the language of human wisdom, in order to make sure that Christ's death on the cross is not robbed of its power.

For the message about Christ's death on the cross is nonsense to those who are being lost; but for us who are being saved it is God's power.

First Letter to the Corinthians, 1

While I was with you, I made up my mind to forget everything except Jesus Christ and especially his death on the cross.

First Letter to the Corinthians, 2

**The peace-maker**

Christ is the visible likeness of the invisible God. He is the first-born Son, superior to all created things. For through him God created everything in heaven and on earth, the seen and the unseen things, including spiritual powers, lords, rulers and authorities. God created the whole universe through him and for him.

Christ existed before all things, and in union with him all things have their proper place. He is the head of his body, the church; he is the source of the body's life. He is the first-born Son, who was raised from death, in order that he alone might have the first place in all things. For it was by God's own decision that the Son has in himself the full nature of God.

Through the Son, then, God decided to bring the whole universe back to himself. God made peace through his Son's death on the cross and so brought back to himself all things, both on earth and in heaven.

Letter to the Colossians, 1

**The truth is – Christ raised from death**

I want to remind you, my brothers of the Good News which I preached to you, which you received, and on which your faith stands

firm. That is the gospel, the message that I preached to you. You are saved by the gospel if you hold firmly to it – unless it was for nothing that you believed.

I passed on to you what I received, which is of the greatest importance: that Christ died for our sins, as written in the Scriptures; that he was buried and that he was raised to life three days later, as written in the Scriptures; that he appeared to Peter and then to all twelve apostles. Then he appeared to more than five hundred of his followers at once, most of whom are still alive ...

Now since our message is that Christ has been raised from death, how can some of you say that the dead will not be raised to life? If that is true, it means that Christ was not raised; and if Christ has not been raised from death, then we have nothing to preach and you have nothing to believe. More than that, we are shown to be lying about God, because we said that he raised Christ from death – but if it is true that the dead are not raised to life, then he did not raise Christ.

For if the dead are not raised, neither has Christ been raised. And if Christ has not been raised, then your faith is a delusion and you are still lost in your sins. It would also mean that the believers in Christ who have died are lost.

If our hope in Christ is good for this life only and no more, then we deserve more pity than anyone else in all the world.

But the truth is that Christ has been raised from death, as the guarantee that those who sleep in death will also be raised.

First Letter to the Corinthians, 15

*On Easter Sunday morning the tomb in which Jesus was buried, with a great stone to seal the entrance, was empty. The whole Christian faith rests on the fact that Jesus is alive. Tombs like this, from the first century and matching the description of the tomb in which Jesus was buried, can still be seen in Israel.*

# PEACE WITH GOD

*Jesus died for us. He endured the separation from God which we deserved because of our disobedience. He secured peace for us. Once we were God's enemies. Now we are his friends.*

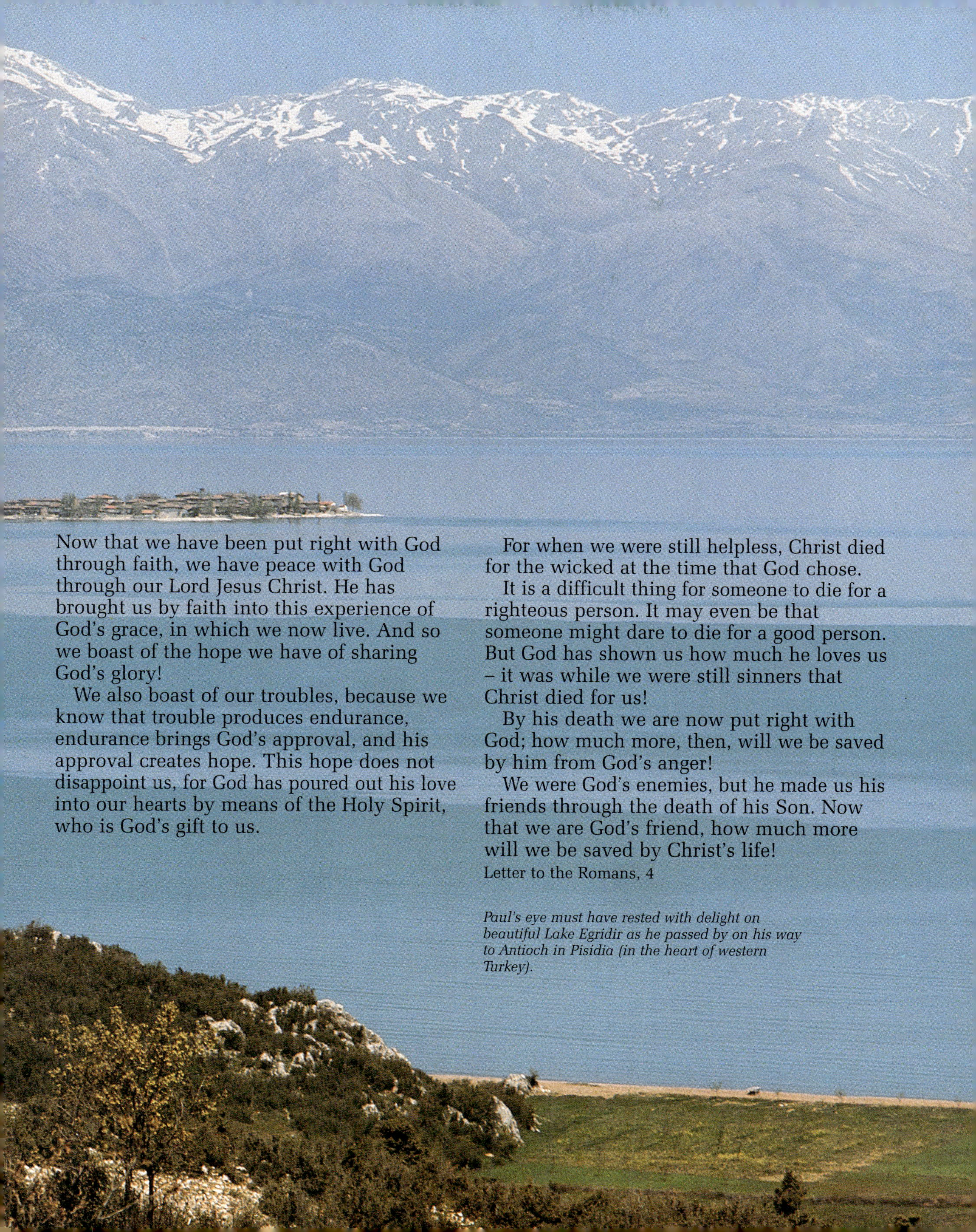

Now that we have been put right with God through faith, we have peace with God through our Lord Jesus Christ. He has brought us by faith into this experience of God's grace, in which we now live. And so we boast of the hope we have of sharing God's glory!

We also boast of our troubles, because we know that trouble produces endurance, endurance brings God's approval, and his approval creates hope. This hope does not disappoint us, for God has poured out his love into our hearts by means of the Holy Spirit, who is God's gift to us.

For when we were still helpless, Christ died for the wicked at the time that God chose.

It is a difficult thing for someone to die for a righteous person. It may even be that someone might dare to die for a good person. But God has shown us how much he loves us – it was while we were still sinners that Christ died for us!

By his death we are now put right with God; how much more, then, will we be saved by him from God's anger!

We were God's enemies, but he made us his friends through the death of his Son. Now that we are God's friend, how much more will we be saved by Christ's life!

Letter to the Romans, 4

*Paul's eye must have rested with delight on beautiful Lake Egridir as he passed by on his way to Antioch in Pisidia (in the heart of western Turkey).*

# A New Life

*God offers us, not just a fresh start with a clean slate, but a new life. When we accept that Christ has died for us, our old life dies with him. As he is raised, we too are given a new life, quite different from the old. Death cannot end it, as it ends our physical life. There is an added dimension, an entirely new quality. Christ lives in us, we share his life, the life of God.*

When we were baptized into union with Christ Jesus, we were baptized into union with his death. By our baptism, then, we were buried with him and shared his death, in order that, just as Christ was raised from death by the glorious power of the Father, so also we might live a new life.

For since we have become one with him in dying as he did, in the same way we shall be one with him by being raised to life as he was. And we know that our old being has been put to death with Christ on his cross, in order that the power of the sinful self might be destroyed, so that we should no longer be the slaves of sin. For when a person dies, he is set free from the power of sin.

Since we have died with Christ, we believe that we will also live with him. For we know that Christ has been raised from death and will never die again – death will no longer rule over him. And so, because he died, sin has no power over him; and now he lives his life in fellowship with God.

In the same way you are to think of yourselves as dead, so far as sin is concerned, but living in fellowship with God through Christ Jesus …

For sin pays its wage – death; but God's free gift is eternal life in union with Christ Jesus our Lord.

Letter to the Romans, 6

## Made new

**When anyone is joined to Christ, he is a new being; the old is gone, the new has come. All this is done by God, who through Christ changed us from enemies into his friends and gave us the task of making others his friends also.**

Second Letter to the Corinthians, 5

*Christ offers us a new life, washed clean from all that lies in the past. It is a life whose keynote is joy.*

# Serving God

*Since we have God's gift of new life, bought at such cost, new thinking and new living are called for.*

**New thinking**

Because of God's great mercy to us I appeal to you: Offer yourselves as a living sacrifice to God, dedicated to his service and pleasing to him. This is the true worship that you should offer. Do not conform yourselves to the standards of this world, but let God transform you inwardly by a complete change of your mind. Then you will be able to know the will of God – what is good and is pleasing to him and is perfect.

And because of God's gracious gift to me I say to every one of you: Do not think of yourself more highly than you should. Instead, be modest in your thinking, and judge yourself according to the amount of faith that God has given you.

We have many parts in the one body, and all these parts have different functions. In the same way, though we are many, we are one body in union with Christ, and we are all joined to each other as different parts of one body. So we are to use our different gifts in accordance with the grace that God has given us.

Letter to the Romans, 12

**Loved and chosen**

You have been raised to life with Christ, so set your hearts on the things that are in heaven, where Christ sits on his throne at the right-hand side of God. Keep your minds fixed on things there, not on things here on earth. For you have died, and your life is hidden with Christ in God. Your real life is Christ and when he appears, then you too will appear with him and share his glory!...

You are the people of God; he loved you and chose you for his own. So then, you must

clothe yourselves with compassion, kindness, humility, gentleness, and patience. Be tolerant with one another and forgive one another whenever any of you has a complaint against someone else. You must forgive one another just as the Lord has forgiven you. And to all these qualities add love, which binds all things together in perfect unity.

The peace that Christ gives is to guide you in the decisions you make; for it is to this peace that God has called you together in the one body. And be thankful.

Christ's message in all its richness must live in your hearts. Teach and instruct each other with all wisdom. Sing psalms, hymns, and sacred songs; sing to God with thanksgiving in your hearts. Everything you do or say, then, should be done in the name of the Lord Jesus, as you give thanks through him to God the Father.

Letter to the Colossians, 3

## The secret

**Don't worry about anything, but in all your prayers ask God for what you need, always asking him with a thankful heart. And God's peace, which is far beyond human understanding, will keep your hearts and minds safe in union with Christ Jesus ...**

**Fill your minds with those things that are good and that deserve praise: things that are true, noble, right, pure, lovely, and honourable. Put into practice what you learnt and received from me, both from my words and from my actions. And the God who gives us peace will be with you.**

Letter to the Philippians, 4

*For every follower of Christ there is work to be done: not simply earning his keep, but living for God in his world.*

# Under New Management

*God asks us, as his people, to model our lives on his. We are to live for him. And we are to show his character – his love, his self-giving, his care – to the world. He is asking the impossible! But we have a 'secret weapon' – the gift of God's Spirit to lead us and help us.*

**Who is in control?**

What I say is this: let the Spirit direct your lives, and you will not satisfy the desires of the human nature. For what our human nature wants is opposed to what the Spirit wants, and what the Spirit wants is opposed to what our human nature wants. These two are enemies, and this means that you cannot do what you want to do. If the Spirit leads you, then you are not subject to the Law.

## The things we share

**Do your best to preserve the unity which the Spirit gives by means of the peace that binds you together.**

**There is one body and one Spirit, just as there is one hope to which God has called you.**

**There is one Lord, one faith, one baptism; there is one God and Father of all mankind, who is Lord of all, works through all, and is in all.**

Letter to the Ephesians, 4

What human nature does is quite plain. It shows itself in immoral, filthy, and indecent actions; in worship of idols and witchcraft. People become enemies and they fight; they become jealous, angry, and ambitious. They separate into parties and groups; they are envious, get drunk, have orgies, and do other things like these. I want you now as I have before, those who do these things will not possess the Kingdom of God.

But the Spirit produces love, joy, peace, patience, kindness, goodness, faithfulness, humility, and self-control. There is no law against such things as these. And those who belong to Christ Jesus have put to death their human nature with all its passions and desires. The Spirit has given us life; he must also control our lives.

Letter to the Galatians, 5

### God's children

Those who are led by God's Spirit are God's sons. For the Spirit that God has given you does not make you slaves and cause you to be afraid; instead, the Spirit makes you God's children, and by the Spirit's power we cry out to God, 'Father! my Father!' God's Spirit joins himself to our spirits to declare that we are God's children.

Since we are his children, we will possess the blessings he keeps for his people, and we will also possess with Christ what God has kept for him; for if we share Christ's suffering, we will also share his glory.

Letter to the Romans, 8

### For the good of all

There are different kinds of spiritual gifts, but the same Spirit gives them. There are different ways of serving, but the same Lord is served. There are different abilities to perform service, but the same God gives ability to everyone for their particular service. The Spirit's presence is shown in some way in each person for the good of all.

The Spirit gives one person a message full of wisdom, while to another person the same Spirit gives a message full of knowledge.

One and the same Spirit gives faith to one person, while to another person he gives the power to heal.

The Spirit gives one person the power to work miracles; to another, the gift of speaking God's message; and to yet another, the ability to tell the difference between gifts that come from the Spirit and those that do not.

To one person he gives the ability to speak in strange tongues, and to another he gives the ability to explain what is said. But it is one and the same Spirit who does all this; as he wishes, he gives a different gift to each person.

First Letter to the Corinthians, 12

*As the tiller controls and directs the boat, so each new Christian comes under the control and direction of the Spirit of God.*

# 'FOR THE GOSPEL'S SAKE'

*Paul could never forget that he had once tried to destroy the church. Those words on the Damascus road – 'I am Jesus, whom you persecute' – rang in his ears. But God had forgiven him. Paul had been given a special mission. From that moment on, he was under 'an obligation to all peoples' to tell them the Good News. Despite danger and hardship, Paul would not spare himself. He would not stand on his rights. He would not count the cost. He would 'become all things to all men' so that, by whatever means, he might 'save some'.*

I have no right to boast just because I preach the gospel. After all, I am under orders to do so. And how terrible it would be for me if I did not preach the gospel! If I did my work as a matter of free choice, then I could expect to be paid; but I do it as a matter of duty, because God has entrusted me with this task. What pay do I get, then? It is the privilege of preaching the Good News without charging for it, without claiming my rights in my work for the gospel.

**Everybody's slave**

I am a free man, nobody's slave; but I make myself everybody's slave in order to win as many people as possible.

While working with the Jews, I live like a Jew in order to win them; and even though I myself am not subject to the Law of Moses, I live as though I were when working with those who are, in order to win them.

In the same way, when working with Gentiles, I live like a Gentile, outside the Jewish Law, in order to win Gentiles. This

## Christ lives in me

**I have been put to death with Christ on his cross, so that it is no longer I who live, but it is Christ who lives in me. This life that I live now, I live by faith in the Son of God, who loved me, and gave his life for me.**
Letter to the Galatians, 2

does not mean that I don't obey God's law; I am really under Christ's law.

Among the weak in faith I become weak like one of them, in order to win them.

So I become all things to all men, that I may save some of them by whatever means are possible.

**To win the prize**

All this I do for the gospel's sake, in order to share in its blessings. Surely you know that many runners take part in a race, but only one of them wins the prize. Run, then, in such a way as to win the prize.

Every athlete in training submits to strict discipline, in order to be crowned with a wreath that will not last; but we do it for one that will last for ever.

First Letter to the Corinthians, 9

*Paul faced danger and hardship to make the gospel known. This famous mountain pass, known as the Cilician Gates, was the traveller's route through the Taurus mountains, near Paul's home town of Tarsus.*

# 'God Knows I Love You!'

*The young churches he brought to birth were in a very real sense Paul's family. He agonized over them as if they were his children. He kept in close touch, both by letter and through his younger colleagues, who were often sent to find out how a particular group was doing, and to give help. Where he saw things that were wrong Paul exercised strong discipline – but always at real personal cost. The men and women in these churches were so close to his heart. He poured out his love for them in constant self-giving. His letters reveal the depth of Paul's feeling – his joy when the Christians stood firm; his deep hurt when there was misunderstanding. 'God knows,' he cries out to the wayward group at Corinth, 'I love you!'*

## The heartache

Dear friends in Corinth! We have spoken frankly to you; we have opened our hearts wide. It is not we who have closed our hearts to you; it is you who have closed your hearts to us. I speak now as though you were my children: show us the same feelings that we have for you. Open your hearts wide!

Second Letter to the Corinthians, 6

Make room for us in your hearts. We have wronged no one; we have ruined no one, nor tried to take advantage of anyone. I do not say this to condemn you; for, as I have said before, you are so dear to us that we are always together, whether we live or die. I am so sure of you; I take such pride in you! In all our troubles I am still full of courage; I am running over with joy.

Even after we arrived in Macedonia, we had no rest. There were troubles everywhere, quarrels with others, fears in our hearts. But God, who encourages the downhearted, encouraged us with the coming of Titus.

It was not only his coming that cheered us, but also his report of how you encouraged him. He told us how much you want to see me, how sorry you are, how ready you are to defend me; and so I am even happier now ...

How happy I am that I can depend on you completely!

Second Letter to the Corinthians 7

## ... and the joy

From Paul, Silas, and Timothy –
To the people of the church in Thessalonica, who belong to God the Father and the Lord Jesus Christ:

May grace and peace be yours.

We always thank God for you all and always mention you in our prayers. For we remember before our God and Father how you put your faith into practice, how your love made you work so hard, and how your hope in our Lord Jesus Christ is firm.

Our brothers, we know that God loves you and has chosen you to be his own. For we brought the Good News to you, not with words only, but also with power and the Holy Spirit, and with complete conviction of its truth.

You know how we lived when we were with you; it was for your own good. You imitated us and the Lord; and even though you suffered much, you received the message with the joy that comes from the Holy Spirit.

So you became an example to all believers in Macedonia and Achaia. For not only did the message about the Lord go out from you throughout Macedonia and Achaia, but the news about your faith in God has gone everywhere.

First Letter to the Thessalonians, 1

*Paul exercised a shepherd's care over the new converts in his young churches.*

# PROFIT AND LOSS

*Paul's relationship with the group of Christians at Philippi was a particularly happy one. It was very much two-way. Knowing that he would never burden a church with his keep, the Philippians gave practical help as he travelled. Their generosity meant all the more because they had so little and it really cost them to give. Paul's letter to the Philippians is warm and personal. Joy is the keynote, even though he writes from prison and is facing possible death. Perhaps it is this which stirs Paul to assess his own life – the loss, and the gain.*

**Living or dying**

I want you to know, my brothers, that the things that have happened to me have really helped the progress of the gospel. As a result, the whole palace guard and all the others here know that I am in prison because I am a servant of Christ …

My deep desire and hope is that I shall never fail in my duty, but that at all times, and especially just now, I shall be full of courage, so that with my whole being I shall bring honour to Christ, whether I live or die.

For what is life? To me, it is Christ. Death, then, will bring more. But if by continuing to live I can do more worthwhile work, then I am not sure which I should choose.

I am pulled in two directions. I want very much to leave this life and be with Christ, which is a far better thing; but for your sake it is much more important that I remain alive …

Letter to the Philippians, 1

**The supreme example**

I urge you, then, to make me completely happy by having the same thoughts, sharing the same love, and being one in soul and mind. Don't do anything from selfish ambition or from a cheap desire to boast, but be humble towards one another, always considering others better than yourselves. And look out for one another's interests, not just for your own.

The attitude you should have is the one that Christ Jesus had:

He always had the nature of God,
but he did not think that by force
he should try to become equal with God.
Instead of this, of his own free will
he gave up all he had,
and took the nature of a servant.
He became like man
and appeared in human likeness.
He was humble and walked the path
of obedience all the way to death –
his death on the cross.
For this reason God raised him to the
highest place above
and gave him the name that is greater
than any other name.
And so, in honour of the name of Jesus
all beings in heaven, on earth, and
in the world below
will fall on their knees,
and all will openly proclaim that
Jesus Christ is Lord,
to the glory of God the Father.

Letter to the Philippians, 2

**Loss and gain**

All those things that I might count as profit I now reckon as loss for Christ's sake. Not only those things; I reckon everything as complete loss for the sake of what is so much more valuable, the knowledge of Christ Jesus my Lord.

For his sake I have thrown everything away; I consider it all as mere refuse, so that I may gain Christ and be completely united with him. I no longer have a righteousness of

*These silver coins from the first and second centuries AD speak both of the cost of the gospel and the generosity of the Christians at Philippi.*

my own, the kind that is gained by obeying the Law. I now have the righteousness that is given through faith in Christ, the righteousness that comes from God and is based on faith.

All I want is to know Christ and to experience the power of his resurrection, to share in his sufferings and become like him in his death, in the hope that I myself will be raised from death to life.

I do not claim that I have already succeeded or have already become perfect. I keep striving to win the prize for which Christ Jesus has already won me to himself. Of course, my brothers, I really do not think that I have already won it; the one thing I do, however, is to forget what is behind me and do my best to reach what is ahead.

So I run straight towards the goal in order to win the prize, which is God's call through Christ Jesus to the life above.

Letter to the Philippians, 3

# Praying Always

*More often than not, as Paul started to write, he penned a prayer. 'God knows that I remember you every time I pray,' he said to the Christians at Rome, whom he had not yet met. When he told new Christians they must pray always he was offering not just advice but personal example, and when Paul prayed it was not simply for practical needs, but that each church would reach out and take hold of God's best.*

**A prayer for wisdom**

Ever since I heard of your faith in the Lord Jesus and your love for all God's people, I have not stopped giving thanks to God for you. I remember you in my prayers and ask the God of our Lord Jesus Christ, the glorious Father, to give you the Spirit, who will make you wise and reveal God to you, so that you will know him.

I ask that your minds may be opened to see his light, so that you will know what is the hope to which he has called you, how rich are the wonderful blessings he promises his people, and how very great is his power at work in us who believe. This power working in us is the same as the mighty strength which he used when he raised Christ from death and seated him at his right hand in the heavenly world.

Letter to the Ephesians, 1

**A prayer for strength**

I ask God from the wealth of his glory to give you power through his Spirit to be strong in your inner selves, and I pray that Christ will make his home in your hearts through faith.

I pray that you may have your roots and foundation in love, so that you, together with all God's people, may have the power to understand how broad and long, how high and deep, is Christ's love. Yes, may you come to know his love – although it can never be fully known – and so be completely filled with the very nature of God.
Letter to the Ephesians, 3

**A prayer for love**

You are always in my heart! ... God is my witness that I am telling the truth when I say that my deep feeling for you all comes from the heart of Christ Jesus himself.

I pray that your love will keep on growing more and more, together with true knowledge and perfect judgement, so that you will be able to choose what is best. Then you will be free from all impurity and blame on the Day of Christ. Your lives will be filled with the truly good qualities which only Jesus Christ can produce, for the glory and praise of God.
Letter to the Philippians, 1

**A prayer for life**

We ask God to fill you with the knowledge of his will, with all the wisdom and understanding that his Spirit gives. Then you will be able to live as the Lord wants and will always do what pleases him. Your lives will produce all kinds of good deeds, and you will grow in your knowledge of God.

May you be made strong with all the strength which comes from his glorious power, so that you may be able to endure everything with patience. And with joy give thanks to the Father, who has made you fit to have your share of what God has reserved for his people in the kingdom of light.
Letter to the Colossians, 1

*The farmer needs patience and perseverance. So too does the Christian, following Paul's example and instruction to 'pray always'.*

# Praise God!

*In Paul's prayers, asking and thanking go together. In his letters, the practical teaching about life and life-style arises out of what God has done. It is because of what he gives us, God's rich blessings, that we are to live for him. Paul's own awareness of the goodness of God was so deep that he often breaks off writing and breaks into praise.*

**God, the Giver**

Let us give thanks to the God and Father of our Lord Jesus Christ! For in our union with Christ he has blessed us by giving us every spiritual blessing in the heavenly world. Even before the world was made, God had already chosen us to be his through our union with Christ, so that we would be holy and without fault before him.

Because of his love God had already decided that through Jesus Christ he would make us his sons – this was his pleasure and purpose. Let us praise God for his glorious grace, for the free gift he gave us in his dear Son! For by the death of Christ we are set free, that is, our sins are forgiven. How great is the grace of God, which he gave to us in such large measure!

In all his wisdom and insight God did what he had purposed, and made known to us the secret plan he had already decided to complete by means of Christ. This plan, which God will complete when the time is right, is to bring all creation together, everything in heaven and on earth, with Christ as head.

All things are done according to God's plan and decision; and God chose us to be his own

people in union with Christ because of his own purpose, based on what he had decided from the very beginning. Let us, then, who were the first to hope in Christ, praise God's glory!
Letter to the Ephesians, 1

### God, the all-wise

Let us give glory to God! He is able to make you stand firm in your faith, according to the Good News I preach about Jesus Christ and according to the revelation of the secret truth which was hidden for long ages in the past. Now, however, that truth has been brought out into the open through the writings of the prophets: and by the command of the eternal God it is made known to all nations, so that all may believe and obey.

To the only God, who alone is all-wise, be glory through Jesus Christ for ever! Amen.
Letter to the Romans, 16

## To God be the glory

**To him who by means of his power working in us is able to do so much more than we can ever ask for, or even think of: to God be the glory in the church and in Christ Jesus for all time, for ever and ever! Amen.**
Letter to the Ephesians, 3

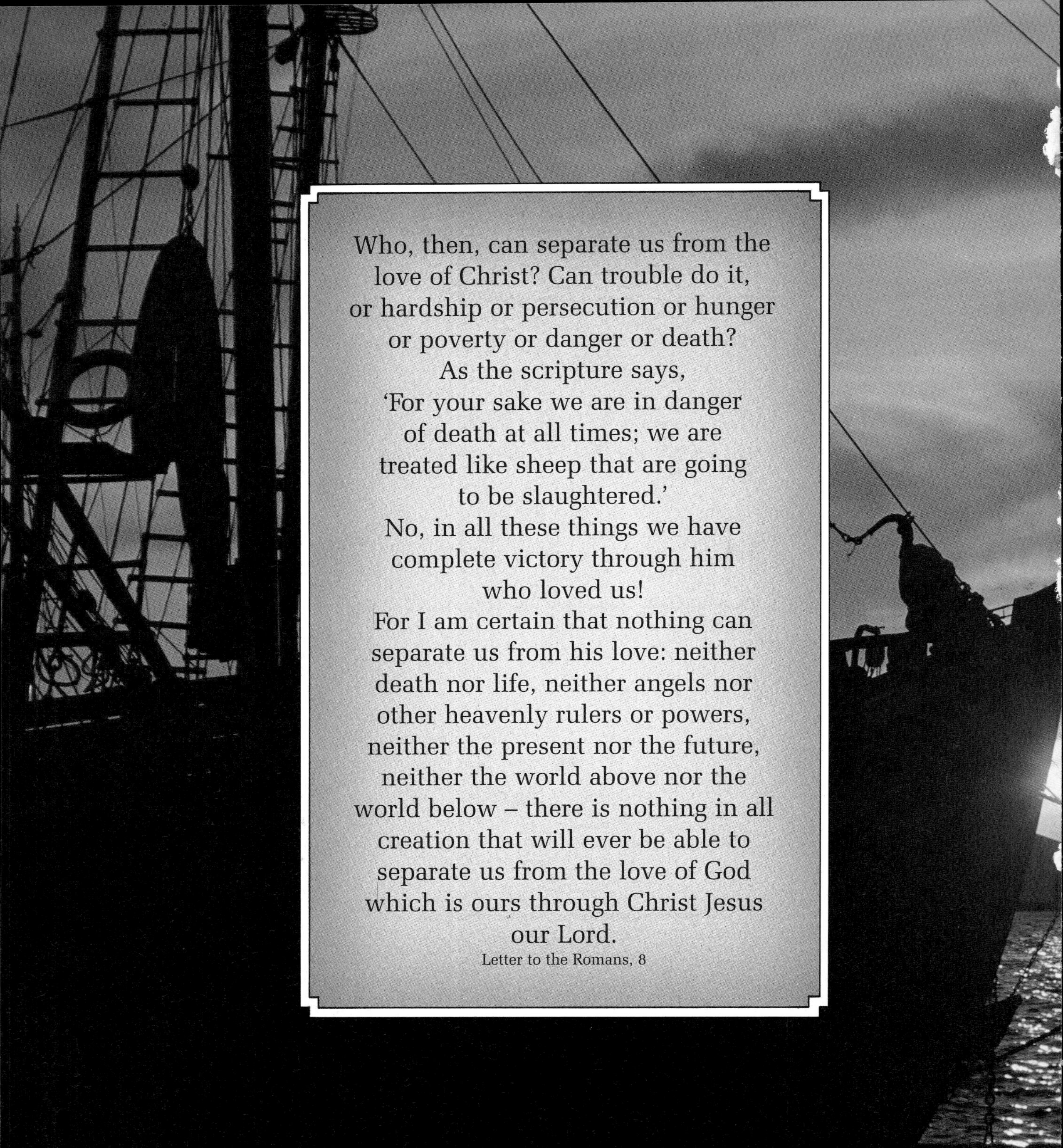

Who, then, can separate us from the
love of Christ? Can trouble do it,
or hardship or persecution or hunger
or poverty or danger or death?
As the scripture says,
'For your sake we are in danger
of death at all times; we are
treated like sheep that are going
to be slaughtered.'
No, in all these things we have
complete victory through him
who loved us!
For I am certain that nothing can
separate us from his love: neither
death nor life, neither angels nor
other heavenly rulers or powers,
neither the present nor the future,
neither the world above nor the
world below – there is nothing in all
creation that will ever be able to
separate us from the love of God
which is ours through Christ Jesus
our Lord.

Letter to the Romans, 8

# PART THREE
## Under Pressure

# Accusation and Arrest

*After the uproar at Ephesus had died down 'Paul called together the believers and with words of encouragement said goodbye to them.' He travelled through Greece strengthening and encouraging the local groups of Christians.*

*He was now in a hurry to get to Jerusalem by the Day of Pentecost – and took ship. The coastal vessel made several ports of call. At Miletus Paul was able to arrange a meeting with church leaders from nearby Ephesus. Paul sensed he would not see them again. God was calling him to Jerusalem and he did not know what would happen there. His one concern was to finish the work he had been given to do. There was an emotional farewell.*

*A few weeks later Paul reached Ptolemais on the coast of Israel. At nearby Caesarea a prophet predicted that Paul would be taken prisoner if he went to Jerusalem. Many were anxious for him. But Paul was determined.*

*The arrest took place. Certain Jews thought Paul had broken the Law by taking one of his Gentile friends into the Temple courts. He appeared before the Council. But there was a plot to kill him and for his own safety Roman soldiers took him under escort to the garrison at Caesarea, where he awaited the judgement of Governor Felix. At last he was given a hearing. Paul began to speak…*

'I know that you have been a judge over this nation for many years, and so I am happy to defend myself before you.

'As you can find out for yourself it was no more than twelve days ago that I went to Jerusalem to worship. The Jews did not find me arguing with anyone in the Temple, nor did they find me stirring up the people, either in the synagogues or anywhere else in the city. Nor can they give you proof of the accusations they now bring against me.

'I do admit this to you: I worship the God of our ancestors by following that Way which they say is false. But I also believe in everything written in the Law of Moses and the books of the prophets. I have the same hope in God that these themselves have, namely, that all people, both the good and the bad, will rise from death. And so I do my best always to have a clear conscience before God and man.

'After being away from Jerusalem for several years, I went there to take some money to my own people and to offer sacrifices. It was while I was doing this that they found me in the Temple after I had completed the ceremony of purification. There was no crowd with me and no disorder. But some Jews from the province of Asia were there; they themselves ought to come before you and make their accusations if they have anything against me. Or let these men here tell what crime they found me guilty of when I stood before the Council – except for the one thing I called out when I stood before them: "I am being tried by you today for believing that the dead will rise to life." '

Then Felix, who was well informed about the Way, brought the hearing to a close.

'When Lysias the commander arrives,' he told them, 'I will decide your case.'

He ordered the officer in charge of Paul to keep him under guard, but to give him some freedom and allow his friends to provide for his needs.

After some days Felix came with his wife Drusilla, who was Jewish. He sent for Paul and listened to him as he talked about faith in Christ Jesus. But as Paul went on discussing about goodness, self-control, and the coming Day of Judgement, Felix was afraid and said, 'You may leave now. I will call you again when I get the chance.'

Acts 24

*Waves dash against the ancient harbour at Caesarea, where Paul was kept prisoner. They wash against fallen Roman pillars.*

# THE APPEAL TO CAESAR

*Two years passed and Paul was still in custody at Caesarea. The new Governor, Porcius Festus, wanted to keep on the right side of the Jews – and they pressed him to return Paul to Jerusalem. They planned to kill Paul on the way. But Paul had the right, as a Roman citizen, to get his case referred to Rome …*

Festus wanted to gain favour with the Jews, so he asked Paul, 'Would you be willing to go to Jerusalem and be tried on these charges before me there?'

Paul said, 'I am standing before the Emperor's own court of judgement, where I should be tried. I have done no wrong to the Jews, as you yourself well know. If I have broken the law and done something for which I deserve the death penalty, I do not ask to escape it. But if there is no truth in the charges they bring against me, no one can hand me over to them. I appeal to the Emperor.'

Then Festus, after conferring with his advisers, answered, 'You have appealed to the Emperor, so to the Emperor you will go.'
Acts 25

*Paul appealed to the Emperor Claudius. His case would be heard in Rome. The Roman forum, with the great Colosseum behind, still stand as reminders of the might of Empire.*

# STORM AND SHIPWRECK

*Agrippa, the provincial king, came on an official visit to welcome the new Governor. Festus spoke to him about the prisoner, Paul. There was still no clear charge against him. Perhaps the Jewish king could help decide. Paul stood before Agrippa and once again spoke in his own defence, telling of his conversion and the work to which God had called him.*

*'Do you think you can make me a Christian?' said the king.*

*'My prayer to God is that you and all the rest of you who are listening to me today might become what I am – except, of course, for these chains,' was Paul's reply.*

*'This man could have been released,' Agrippa said to Festus, 'if he had not appealed to the Emperor.'*

*So Paul set sail for Rome. By the time they reached Crete it was early October. The weather was unpredictable. It would have been sensible to winter on the island. Paul warned of the danger. But the men wanted to move to a better harbour. Luke, who was with Paul, tells what happened …*

A soft wind from the south began to blow, and the men thought that they could carry out their plan, so they pulled up the anchor and sailed as close as possible along the coast of Crete.

But soon a very strong wind – the one called 'North-easter' – blew down from the island. It hit the ship, and since it was impossible to keep the ship headed into the wind, we gave up trying and let it be carried along by the wind.

We got some shelter when we passed to the south of the little island of Cauda. There, with some difficulty, we managed to make the ship's boat secure. They pulled it aboard and then fastened some ropes tight round the ship.

They were afraid that they might run into the sandbanks off the coast of Libya, so they lowered the sail and let the ship be carried by the wind.

The violent storm continued, so on the next day they began to throw some of the ship's cargo overboard, and on the following day they threw part of the ship's equipment overboard.

For many days we could not see the sun or the stars, and the wind kept on blowing very hard. We finally gave up all hope of being saved.

After the men had gone a long time without food, Paul stood before them and said, 'Men, you should have listened to me and not have sailed from Crete; then we would have avoided all this damage and loss. But now I beg you, take heart! Not one of you will lose his life; only the ship will be lost. For last night an angel of the God to whom I belong and whom I worship came to me and said, "Don't be afraid, Paul! You must stand before the Emperor. And God in his goodness to you has spared the lives of all those who are sailing with you." So take heart, men! For I trust in God that it will be just as I was told. But we will be driven ashore on some island.'

It was the fourteenth night, and we were being driven about in the Mediterranean by the storm. About midnight the sailors suspected that we were getting close to land. So they dropped a line with a weight tied to it and found that the water was forty metres deep; a little later they did the same and found that it was thirty metres deep.

They were afraid that the ship would go on the rocks, so they lowered four anchors from the back of the ship and prayed for daylight ...

When the day came, the sailors did not recognize the coast, but they noticed a bay with a beach and decided that, if possible, they would run the ship aground there.

So they cut off the anchors and let them sink in the sea, and at the same time they untied the ropes that held the steering oars. Then they raised the sail at the front of the ship so that the wind would blow the ship forward, and we headed for shore.

But the ship hit a sandbank and went aground; the front part of the ship got stuck and could not move, while the back part was being broken to pieces by the violence of the waves.

The soldiers made a plan to kill all the prisoners, in order to keep them from swimming ashore and escaping. But the army officer wanted to save Paul, so he stopped them from doing this. Instead, he ordered all the men who could swim to jump overboard first and swim ashore; the rest were to follow, holding on to the planks or to some broken pieces of the ship.

And this was how we all got safely ashore.

Acts 27

*Paul was on his way to Rome for trial when his ship struck a sandbank off Malta and sank. It was thanks to Paul that no one was lost.*

# Rome at Last!

*The sandbank on which Paul's ship foundered was on the coast of Malta. The local people welcomed the shivering survivors and lit a fire to warm them. Three months later they boarded a ship from Alexandria which had spent the winter at the island. And so they came to Rome. To Paul's joy Christians from Rome, whom he had so longed to meet, came out along the Appian Way to walk with him the last few miles. And so he had his first sight of the city, set on its seven hills – the magnificent buildings, villas and gardens; the stinking slums. Here a million free citizens were served by an equal number of slaves. All night long carts from the country rattled over the cobbles. By day the streets were packed with jostling people. Crowds at the Circus Maximus roared their applause for the charioteers. Rome at last! And for Paul a new opportunity to declare the Good News about Jesus.*

When we arrived in Rome, Paul was allowed to live by himself with a soldier guarding him.

After three days Paul called the local Jewish leaders to a meeting. When they had gathered, he said to them, 'My fellow-Israelites, even though I did nothing against our people or the customs that we received from our ancestors, I was made a prisoner in Jerusalem and handed over to the Romans. After questioning me, the Romans wanted to release me, because they found that I had done nothing for which I deserved to die. But when the Jews opposed this, I was forced to appeal to the Emperor, even though I had no accusation to make against my own people. That is why I asked to see you and talk with you. As a matter of fact, I am bound in chains like this for the sake of him for whom the people of Israel hope.'

They said to him, 'We have not received any letters from Judaea about you, nor have any of our people come from there with any news or anything bad to say about you. But we would like to hear your ideas, because we know that everywhere people speak against this party to which you belong.'

So they fixed a date with Paul, and a large number of them came that day to the place where Paul was staying. From morning till night he explained to them his message about the Kingdom of God, and he tried to convince them about Jesus by quoting from the Law of Moses and the writings of the prophets. Some of them were convinced by his words, but others would not believe.

Paul concluded: 'You are to know, then, that God's message of salvation has been sent to the Gentiles. They will listen!'

For two years Paul lived in a place he

## Paul's longing to visit Rome

**I have been prevented many times from coming to you. But now that I have finished my work in these regions and since I have been wanting for so many years to come to see you, I hope to do so now ...**

**I urge you, brothers, by our Lord Jesus Christ and by the love that the Spirit gives: join me in praying fervently to God for me. Pray that I may be kept safe from the unbelievers in Judaea and that my service in Jerusalem may be acceptable to God's people there. And so I will come to you full of joy, if it is God's will, and enjoy a refreshing visit to you. May God, our source of peace, be with all of you. Amen.**

Letter to the Romans, 15

rented for himself, and there he welcomed all who came to see him. He preached about the Kingdom of God and taught about the Lord Jesus Christ, speaking with all boldness and freedom.
Luke's words, in Acts 28

*Paul came to Rome along the ancient Appian Way. The Colosseum, floodlit here, is silent witness to the fact that Rome had a cruel way with prisoners.*

# Sharing Christ's Suffering

*At the time of Paul's conversion, Jesus himself had spoken these words to the fearful Ananias: 'I myself will show him all that he must suffer for my sake.'*
*Jesus paid for our forgiveness and peace with his life's blood. Paul and his fellow-apostles were called to share in his sufferings in order to bring the Good News to needy men and women.*
*'The scars I have on my body show that I am the slave of Jesus,' Paul wrote to the Galatian Christians.*

**A public spectacle**

It seems to me that God has given the very last place to us apostles, like men condemned to die in public as a spectacle for the whole world of angels and of mankind. For Christ's sake we are fools; but you are wise in union with Christ! We are weak, but you are strong! We are despised, but you are honoured! To this very moment we go hungry and thirsty; we are clothed in rags; we are beaten; we wander from place to place; we wear ourselves out with hard work. When we are

cursed, we bless; when we are persecuted, we endure; when we are insulted, we answer with kind words. We are no more than this world's refuse; we are the scum of the earth to this very moment!
First Letter to the Corinthians, 4

**Enduring trouble**

In everything we do we show that we are God's servants by patiently enduring troubles, hardships, and difficulties.

We have been beaten, imprisoned, and mobbed; we have been overworked and have gone without sleep or food.

By our purity, knowledge, patience, and kindness we have shown ourselves to be God's servants – by the Holy Spirit, by our true love, by our message of truth, and by the power of God. We have righteousness as our weapon, both to attack and to defend ourselves.

We are honoured and disgraced; we are insulted and praised. We are treated as liars, yet we speak the truth; as unknown, yet we are known by all; as though we were dead, but, as you see, we live on.

Although punished, we are not killed; although saddened, we are always glad; we seem poor, but we make many people rich; we seem to have nothing, yet we really possess everything.
Second Letter to the Corinthians, 6

**In danger and distress**

Five times I was given the thirty-nine lashes by the Jews; three times I was whipped by the Romans; and once I was stoned. I have been in three shipwrecks, and once I spent twenty-four hours in the water. In my many travels I have been in danger from floods and from robbers, in danger from fellow-Jews and from Gentiles; there have been dangers in the cities, dangers in the wilds, dangers on the high seas, and dangers from false friends.

There has been work and toil; often I have gone without sleep; I have been hungry and thirsty; I have often been without enough food, shelter, or clothing.

## When I am weak, then I am strong

*On top of all his other hardships Paul endured the wearing pain of a chronic physical disability. Three times he pleaded with God for healing. But God did not take the pain away.*

**His answer was: 'My grace is all you need, for my power is strongest when you are weak.' I am most happy, then, to be proud of my weaknesses, in order to feel the protection of Christ's power over me. I am content with weaknesses, insults, hardships, persecutions, and difficulties for Christ's sake. For when I am weak, then I am strong.**
Second Letter to the Corinthians, 12

And not to mention other things, every day I am under the pressure of my concern for all the churches. When someone is weak, then I feel weak too; when someone is led into sin, I am filled with distress.
Second Letter to the Corinthians, 11

# LOOKING FORWARD

*We do not know what happened when Paul's case came before the Emperor Nero. Most likely it was dismissed, leaving Paul a few more years in which to make the gospel known and see his young churches firmly established.*

*If this is so, Paul was arrested again. All the traditions say that he died for his faith during Nero's terrible persecutions – in about* AD *64. Some say Peter and Paul died the same day, one crucified upside-down, the other, because he was a Roman citizen, beheaded by the executioner's sword.*

*What is certain is that Paul had long faced death. He looked forward eagerly to being with Christ, which was 'far better'. His hope was firm. He had fought a good fight. He had kept the faith.*

**Creation restored**

I consider that what we suffer at this present time cannot be compared at all with the glory that is going to be revealed to us.

All of creation waits with eager longing for God to reveal his sons. For creation was condemned to lose its purpose, not of its own will, but because God willed it to be so. Yet there was the hope that creation itself would one day be set free from its slavery to decay and should share the glorious freedom of the children of God. For we know that up to the present time all of creation groans with pain, like the pain of childbirth.

But it is not just creation alone which groans; we who have the Spirit as the first of God's gifts also groan within ourselves, as we wait for God to make us his sons and set our whole being free.

For it was by hope that we were saved; but if we see what we hope for, then it is not really hope. For who hopes for something he sees? But if we hope for what we do not see, we wait for it with patience.

In the same way the Spirit also comes to help us, weak as we are. For we do not know how we ought to pray; the Spirit himself pleads with God for us in groans that words

cannot express. And God, who sees into our hearts, knows what the thought of the Spirit is; because the Spirit pleads with God on behalf of his people and in accordance with his will.

We know that in all things God works for good with those who love him, those whom he has called according to his purpose.

Those whom God had already chosen he also set apart to become like his Son, so that the Son would be the first among many brothers. And so those whom God set apart, he called; and those he called, he put right with himself, and he shared his glory with them.

The Letter to the Romans, 8

**With Jesus, always**

We believe that Jesus died and rose again, and so we believe that God will take back with Jesus those who have died believing in him.

What we are teaching you now is the Lord's teaching: we who are alive on the day the Lord comes will not go ahead of those who have died. There will be the shout of command, the archangel's voice, the sound of God's trumpet, and the Lord himself will come down from heaven. Those who have died believing in Christ will rise to life first; then we who are living at that time will be gathered up along with them in the clouds to meet the Lord in the air. And so we will always be with the Lord.

First Letter to the Thessalonians, 4

## A glorious future

**Even though our physical being is gradually decaying, yet our spiritual being is renewed day after day. And this small and temporary trouble we suffer will bring us a tremendous and eternal glory, much greater than the trouble. For we fix our attention, not on things that are seen, but on things that are unseen. What can be seen lasts only for a time, but what cannot be seen lasts for ever.**

Second Letter to the Corinthians, 4

The time is here for me to leave this life. I have done my best in the race, I have run the full distance, and I have kept the faith. And now there is waiting for me the prize of victory awarded for a righteous life, the prize which the Lord, the righteous Judge, will give me on that Day – and not only to me, but to all those who wait with love for him to appear.

Second Letter to Timothy, 4